HOW TO USE LASER ENGRAVER FOR BEGINNER

Unlocking Your Artistic Potential with Lasers

Peter L. Baxley

Copyright © 2024 by Peter L. Baxley

All rights reserved

No part of this publication may be reproduced, stored in a retrieval system. or transmitted. in and form or by any means, electronic, mechanical, photocopying, recoraing, or otherwise, without the prior written permission of the author. The information in this ebook is true and complete to the best of our knowledge. All recommendations are made without guarantee on the part of the author or publisher. The author and publisher disclaim any liability in connection with the use of this information.

Table of Contents

Introduction to Laser Engraving 4

    What is Laser Engraving? 7

    Types of Laser Engravers 10

    Benefits of Laser Engraving 13

    Applications of Laser Engraving 16

Safety First: Understanding Laser Engraver Safety 20

    Basic Safety Guidelines 20

    Personal Protective Equipment (PPE) 23

    Understanding Laser Classification 26

    Workspace Setup for Safety 29

Getting Started with Your Laser Engraver 33

    Unboxing and Setting Up 33

    Understanding Your Laser Engraver's Parts 36

    Initial Machine Calibration 39

    Choosing the Right Material for Your Project 42

Software and Design Basics 46

    Choosing the Right Software 46

    Designing for Laser Engraving: Tips and Tricks 49

    Preparing Your Design for Engraving 52

    Testing Your Design on Different Materials 55

Operating Your Laser Engraver 59

Step-by-Step Guide to Your First Engraving 59

Material Placement and Focus Adjustment 62

Configuring Power, Speed, and Resolution 65

Troubleshooting Common Issues 68

Advanced Techniques and Tips 71

Engraving Different Materials (Wood, Acrylic, Metal, Glass) 71

Multi-Layered Engraving 74

Using Jigs for Batch Production 77

Tips for Improving Engraving Quality 80

Maintenance and Care of Your Laser Engraver 83

Daily and Weekly Maintenance Routines 83

Cleaning and Replacing the Laser Lens 86

Maintaining the Laser Tube 89

Troubleshooting Mechanical Issues 92

Creative Projects to Get You Started 96

Simple Projects for Beginners 96

Intermediate Projects to Explore 99

Advanced Project Ideas 102

Conclusion 105

Introduction to Laser Engraving

In the bustling heart of a small town, nestled among quaint little shops and vibrant cafés, there was an artisan known for her extraordinary creations. Mia, with her warm smile and skillful hands, crafted pieces that seemed to whisper stories of old. Yet, as her reputation grew, so did her ambition. She longed to etch her tales not just in the minds of her patrons but onto the very essence of her creations. That's when she encountered the world of laser engraving.

Despite her excitement, Mia quickly realized that mastering a laser engraver was no simple task. The machine, with its buttons and levers and a beam as fine as a strand of silk, seemed to speak a language all its own. Her first attempts were humble, marked by errors and the occasional burnt edge. It was a dance of power and precision she had yet to master.

One day, as she wandered through the pages of an online store, a title caught her eye: "How to Use a Laser Engraver for Beginners." The cover, adorned with intricate patterns etched in wood, metal, and glass, promised the knowledge she sought. On a whim, fueled by hope and a touch of desperation, she bought the book.

The book was a revelation. It began with a gentle introduction to the art of laser engraving, weaving history with practical advice. Mia learned not just of the machine but of the passion that had driven inventors and artists alike. She discovered the types of laser engravers, each suited to different materials and dreams. The safety chapter was a stark reminder of the respect and care required in this craft, transforming her apprehension into confidence.

As Mia delved deeper, the book offered a lantern in the dark. The software and design basics chapter became her bible, guiding her through the labyrinth of digital art preparation. She practiced, her workshop alight with the soft glow of the computer screen as she translated her visions into digital form.

Then came the heart of the journey: operating the laser engraver. The book laid out a step-by-step guide, from the initial setup to the final masterpiece. Each page was a treasure trove of tips, from adjusting the focus to selecting the right power and speed. Mia's hands, once unsure, now moved with purpose, guiding the laser as it danced across surfaces, etching her stories in lines of light.

With each chapter, her skills flourished. She explored advanced techniques, delved into maintenance and care, and even dreamed of expanding her craft into a business. The book was more than a manual; it was a mentor, guiding her through mistakes and celebrating her successes.

Her creations, once simple, now carried the depth of her tales, etched in intricate detail. Patrons marveled at the transformation, their eyes tracing the lines that told stories of love, adventure, and wonder. Mia's shop became a beacon for those seeking not just a gift but a piece of art that held a piece of the soul.

"Why should you buy this book?" Mia would say, her eyes alight with the passion of a thousand stories yet to be told. "Because within these pages lies not just the key to mastering a tool, but the doorway to a world where your art can speak, breathe, and live. It's not just about learning a skill; it's about unlocking the stories etched in your heart."

And so, the book, "How to Use a Laser Engraver for Beginners," became not just a guide but a symbol of the journey from novice to artisan, a testament to the magic that lies in the marriage of technology and artistry. For Mia, and for all who followed in her footsteps, it was the first step into a world where every creation whispered tales of wonder, waiting for those brave enough to etch them into being.

What is Laser Engraving?

Laser engraving stands as a pinnacle of modern technology's intersection with the timeless desire for personalization and artistic expression. At its core, this process utilizes a highly focused beam of light - the laser - to precisely remove material from the surface of an object, creating images, text, or patterns. Unlike traditional methods that rely on tools or ink, laser engraving offers unmatched precision and versatility, allowing for detailed and complex designs on a wide array of materials including wood, acrylic, metal, glass, and even leather.

The essence of laser engraving lies in its ability to vaporize or ablate the material where the laser beam contacts the surface, leaving behind a permanent mark that is both tactile and visually striking. This is achieved through the laser's intense heat, which can be finely controlled and directed with computer software. This software component is crucial, as it converts digital designs into reality, guiding the laser across the surface of the material in a predetermined path that mirrors the intricacies of the original design.

For beginners, understanding the technology behind laser engraving is the first step towards harnessing its full potential. The process begins with the creation or selection of a design in a digital format. This design is then imported into engraving software, which translates it into a language the laser engraver can interpret. The material to be engraved is prepared and placed within the engraver, where adjustments such as focusing the laser and setting the speed and power are made. These settings are pivotal; they determine the depth of the engraving, the precision of the details, and the overall quality of the finished piece.

Laser engraving's appeal to beginners and seasoned professionals alike stems from its non-contact nature, which minimizes wear and tear on the tools and allows for the consistent production of identical pieces. Furthermore, the process is relatively clean and efficient, with many modern laser engravers equipped with systems to extract fumes and debris.

Safety is a paramount concern when operating a laser engraver. The intense light can pose risks to eyesight and skin, necessitating the use of protective eyewear and adherence to safety guidelines. Moreover, understanding the properties of different materials is crucial, as some can release harmful fumes when engraved.

One of the most exciting aspects of laser engraving for beginners is the breadth of creativity it unlocks. From personalized jewelry and custom signage to intricate artwork and unique gifts, the possibilities are boundless. Additionally, as skills advance, laser engraving can evolve into a lucrative business venture, offering services ranging from bespoke products to industrial part marking.

Laser engraving is a fascinating blend of art and science, offering a gateway to endless creative exploration. For those embarking on this journey, mastering the laser engraver begins with a deep understanding of its workings, safety measures, and the endless potential it holds for transforming ordinary objects into extraordinary creations. With patience, practice, and a spirit of innovation, beginners can not only master the technique but also carve out their niche in the vast world of laser-engraved art and products.

Types of Laser Engravers

Laser engravers, versatile tools in the realm of manufacturing and artistic creation, come in various types, each suited to specific materials and applications, making them an essential topic for beginners. The primary distinction among laser engravers lies in the source of the laser: CO2, fiber, and diode lasers, each with unique characteristics and uses.

CO2 laser engravers are the most commonly used type, favored for their versatility. These machines utilize a carbon dioxide gas mixture, energized by electrical discharges, to produce a laser beam capable of cutting and engraving a wide range of materials, including wood, acrylic, glass, leather, and some types of plastics. The strength of CO2 lasers, typically ranging from 40W to over 150W, allows for both detailed engraving and efficient cutting, making them ideal for hobbyists and professionals in industries such as signage, decoration, and product customization.

Fiber laser engravers, on the other hand, shine in their ability to process metals and engineered plastics. They generate a laser beam through the use of rare-earth elements like ytterbium, which is amplified in a fiber optic cable. Fiber lasers are known for their precision, speed, and efficiency, particularly in marking metals like steel, aluminum, copper, and brass, as well as materials like anodized aluminum and certain plastics. These lasers are highly valued in the automotive, electronics, and medical device industries for tasks requiring durability and resistance to abrasion and chemicals.

Diode laser engravers represent a more accessible entry point for beginners and hobbyists, thanks to their compact size and affordability. Diode lasers use semiconductor technology to produce a laser beam, with power outputs typically ranging from 1W to 20W. While not as powerful as CO2 or fiber lasers, diode lasers are capable of engraving on wood, leather, acrylic, and certain metals when used with a marking compound. Their portability and ease of use make diode laser engravers a popular choice for small-scale projects, personalization, and educational purposes.

Each type of laser engraver requires understanding its capabilities, limitations, and the optimal settings for different materials. CO2 lasers, with their broad material compatibility, are excellent for general-purpose engraving and cutting. Fiber lasers are indispensable for industrial applications involving metal marking and engraving. Diode lasers, while less powerful, offer a cost-effective solution for beginners and enthusiasts looking to explore the world of laser engraving without a significant investment.

Beyond the laser source, factors such as work area size, laser power, software compatibility, and safety features play a critical role in selecting the right laser engraver. A thorough understanding of these types and their applications empowers beginners to make informed decisions, ensuring they choose a machine that best suits their creative or professional needs. As users gain experience, they can explore the diverse capabilities of these lasers, from simple engravings to intricate cuts and marks, unlocking the full potential of laser engraving in their projects.

Benefits of Laser Engraving

Laser engraving, a technology revered for its precision and versatility, offers numerous benefits, particularly appealing to beginners eager to explore the realms of creativity and craftsmanship. This method, utilizing a laser to etch designs onto various materials, stands out for its precision. Unlike traditional manual engraving, laser engravers can achieve intricate details with utmost accuracy, making even the most complex patterns possible without the need for physical contact with the material. This aspect not only preserves the integrity of delicate materials but also opens up a world of design possibilities that were once deemed too challenging for novice hands.

One of the significant advantages of laser engraving is its versatility. A beginner can work across a wide array of materials including wood, acrylic, metal, glass, and even leather, each offering a unique canvas for creativity. This versatility allows newcomers to experiment and find their niche or preferred medium without the need for multiple, specialized tools. Moreover, the ability to quickly switch between materials and projects without extensive setup changes encourages exploration and learning, accelerating the journey from novice to skilled artisan.

Efficiency and speed are also key benefits. Laser engravers, guided by computer software, can complete intricate designs in minutes, a task that might take hours by hand. This efficiency is not just about speed but also about the repeatability of high-quality results. Beginners can produce multiple copies of their work with consistent quality, making laser engraving ideal for small-scale production or personal projects that require uniformity.

The non-contact nature of laser engraving ensures minimal wear and tear on tools and materials. Traditional engraving methods can lead to tool degradation and material damage over time, but laser engravers eliminate this issue, extending the lifespan of both the engraver and the materials used. This aspect is particularly beneficial for beginners, as it reduces the need for frequent tool replacement and material waste, ensuring a smoother learning curve and more sustainable practice.

Safety, while often overlooked, is a paramount benefit. Laser engraving, when operated under proper safety guidelines, poses less risk of physical injury compared to manual engraving tools. The enclosed design of most laser engravers minimizes the risk of direct contact with the laser, making it a safer alternative for those new to the craft.

The adaptability of laser engravers to computer-aided design (CAD) software is another advantage. This compatibility allows beginners to venture into digital design, offering a more forgiving platform for trial and error. With CAD software, designs can be edited and perfected before engraving, reducing material waste and allowing for easy adjustments. This integration of technology not only enhances creativity but also teaches valuable digital skills that are applicable in various design and manufacturing fields.

Environmental impact is a consideration in any craft, and laser engraving offers benefits in this area as well. The precision of laser engraving reduces material waste, as designs can be placed efficiently to maximize the use of each piece. Furthermore, the process itself is clean, with many laser engravers equipped with systems to filter out any fumes or debris, making it a more environmentally friendly option compared to some traditional methods that can produce significant waste and pollution.

Lastly, the personal satisfaction and potential for business development cannot be understated. Beginners can quickly see their ideas come to life, providing immediate gratification and encouragement to continue exploring. As skills develop, laser engraving offers a pathway to entrepreneurship, allowing artisans to sell their work, customize products, or even offer engraving services. This aspect opens up a new dimension for hobbyists, turning a passion into a potential livelihood.

In essence, laser engraving offers a gateway into the world of design and craftsmanship that is accessible, efficient, and rewarding. Its benefits span from the technical, such as precision and versatility, to the personal and economic, offering a comprehensive suite of advantages that appeal to beginners eager to embark on their creative journey.

Applications of Laser Engraving

Laser engraving, a technique that utilizes a high-powered laser beam to etch designs onto various materials, has revolutionized the way we create and customize objects. This technology offers precision and versatility, making it a favorite among hobbyists, artisans, and industrial manufacturers alike. For beginners eager to explore the possibilities of laser engraving, understanding its applications is the first step towards harnessing its full potential.

In the realm of personalization, laser engraving stands unparalleled. It allows for the customization of everyday items such as phone cases, jewelry, and wallets, transforming ordinary objects into unique personal statements or gifts. The precision of the laser beam ensures that even the most intricate designs are possible, enabling the creation of highly detailed and personalized items that reflect individual tastes or commemorate special occasions.

Art and design enthusiasts find laser engraving an invaluable tool for expressing creativity. Artists can transfer their intricate designs onto materials like wood, acrylic, and metal, creating stunning pieces of art that showcase detailed patterns and textures impossible to achieve through traditional methods. This technology has opened new avenues for artistic expression, from intricate wall hangings to bespoke furniture, allowing artists to push the boundaries of their creativity.

In the world of fashion, laser engraving is used to create unique wearable art. Designers engrave intricate patterns onto leather goods, such as belts and handbags, and even onto fabrics, offering a new dimension to textile design. This application not only enhances the aesthetic appeal of fashion items but also allows for the creation of signature pieces that stand out in the competitive fashion market.

The industrial sector benefits significantly from laser engraving, where it is used for the functional marking of parts and tools. Serial numbers, barcodes, and logos can be permanently etched onto products, ensuring traceability and brand recognition. This application is crucial in industries requiring stringent quality control and regulatory compliance, as it provides a non-removable identifier that can withstand harsh conditions without fading or wearing off.

In electronics, laser engraving is employed to label components with identifiers and instructions, contributing to both the functionality and aesthetics of electronic devices. This precise application allows for the miniaturization of components without sacrificing readability, a critical factor in the ever-evolving electronics industry.

The medical field utilizes laser engraving for the marking of surgical instruments and medical devices. Engraved markings ensure that equipment can be easily identified, tracked, and maintained, which is essential for patient safety and the efficiency of medical procedures. The non-contact nature of laser engraving means that delicate instruments can be marked without risk of damage, maintaining their sterility and integrity.

Educationally, laser engraving serves as a hands-on learning tool, introducing students to the principles of design, engineering, and manufacturing. Schools and universities incorporate laser engraving projects into their curriculum, allowing students to explore the intersection of technology and creativity, and to understand the practical applications of their designs in the real world.

In the world of marketing and branding, companies leverage laser engraving to create promotional items and corporate gifts. The ability to customize items with logos, slogans, and designs helps businesses establish their brand identity and leave a lasting impression on clients and partners.

For hobbyists and DIY enthusiasts, laser engraving has democratized the ability to create professional-looking projects at home. From personalized home décor to custom-made gifts, the application of laser engraving in personal projects encourages creativity and personal expression, making the technology accessible and enjoyable for users of all skill levels.

Understanding the diverse applications of laser engraving empowers beginners to explore the vast potential of this technology. Whether for personal projects, artistic expression, industrial use, or educational purposes, laser engraving offers a world of possibilities, making it a valuable skill for anyone interested in the intersection of technology and creativity.

Safety First: Understanding Laser Engraver Safety

Basic Safety Guidelines

When diving into the world of laser engraving, it's paramount to prioritize safety. The use of high-powered lasers carries inherent risks, not just to the user but also to bystanders and the environment. Understanding and adhering to basic safety guidelines can mitigate these risks, ensuring a safe and enjoyable experience for everyone involved.

The first step in laser engraver safety is understanding the equipment. Different types of laser engravers emit varying levels of radiation, and it's crucial to know the class of your laser. Class 4 lasers, commonly used in engraving, are capable of causing damage to skin and eyes on direct contact. Familiarizing yourself with your machine's specifications and safety features is essential.

Eye protection is non-negotiable when operating a laser engraver. The intense light produced by the laser can cause serious eye injuries, even from reflected or scattered light. Wearing safety goggles specifically designed to filter out the wavelength of your laser prevents accidental exposure. Ensure that anyone else in the vicinity also wears appropriate eye protection.

A well-ventilated workspace is vital to avoid exposure to fumes and particulate matter produced during the engraving process. Materials like plastics and certain woods can release harmful chemicals when engraved. Using a fume extractor or ensuring adequate airflow in your engraving area can help maintain a safe breathing environment.

Understanding the materials you are engraving is another crucial aspect of safety. Some materials, such as PVC, release toxic chlorine gas when engraved, which can be harmful to both the operator and the laser equipment. Always research your materials beforehand and consult safety datasheets to determine whether they are safe to engrave.

Proper machine maintenance is a key safety practice. Regularly cleaning and inspecting your laser engraver for damage or wear, especially in critical components like the laser tube and mirrors, ensures that the machine operates within safety parameters. A well-maintained machine is less likely to malfunction, reducing the risk of accidents.

Training and education cannot be overstated. Before operating a laser engraver, one should thoroughly understand its functions, limitations, and emergency procedures. Many manufacturers and community workshops offer training sessions. Taking advantage of these resources can equip you with the knowledge to operate your machine safely.

Emergency preparedness is also part of basic safety guidelines. Ensure you know how to quickly shut down your laser engraver in case of an emergency. Keeping a fire extinguisher rated for electrical fires within easy reach is wise, as is familiarizing yourself with its use.

Lastly, personal responsibility plays a significant role in safety. Never leave the laser engraver unattended while it's in operation. The risk of fire is a reality with laser engraving, and immediate intervention can prevent disaster. Additionally, wearing appropriate clothing and removing any flammable materials from the engraving area can further reduce risks.

By adhering to these basic safety guidelines, beginners can safely explore the creative and professional possibilities offered by laser engraving. Safety practices should be ingrained from the very start, ensuring that as your skills and ambitions grow, so does your commitment to operating safely. This not only protects you but also those around you, fostering a responsible and safety-conscious engraving community.

Personal Protective Equipment (PPE)

When venturing into the realm of laser engraving, a technology that allows for precision cutting and marking on various materials, safety should be a top priority, especially for beginners. Understanding and utilizing Personal Protective Equipment (PPE) is crucial in safeguarding against potential hazards associated with laser engravers. These machines, while invaluable for their precision and versatility, emit high-intensity laser beams capable of causing serious injury or damage if proper precautions are not taken.

One of the primary concerns when operating laser engravers is the risk of eye injury. The intense light produced by the laser can lead to permanent eye damage or blindness if the eyes are not properly protected. Safety glasses or goggles designed specifically to shield against the laser's wavelength are essential. These glasses are not your ordinary eyewear; they are made from special materials that can absorb or reflect the laser light, significantly reducing the risk of eye exposure to harmful rays.

In addition to eye protection, skin protection is also necessary. Even though the laser beam is primarily focused on the material being engraved, reflections or scattered light can still pose a risk to exposed skin. Wearing long-sleeved shirts and gloves can provide an additional layer of safety, especially when working with materials that may emit harmful vapors or particles upon being engraved. It's important to choose gloves that are suitable for the type of material being handled, as some materials may require specific types of gloves to prevent skin irritation or burns.

The materials processed by laser engravers can sometimes release fumes and particles that are harmful when inhaled. Respiratory protection, such as masks or respirators, becomes critical in such scenarios, especially when engraving plastics, coated metals, or any material treated with chemicals. A well-ventilated workspace is essential to ensure these fumes are effectively removed from the breathing area, but personal respiratory equipment can provide an additional safety measure, filtering out harmful particles and ensuring clean air intake.

Hearing protection may also be necessary, particularly with larger industrial laser engravers that generate significant noise during operation. Prolonged exposure to high noise levels can lead to hearing impairment, making earplugs or earmuffs an important part of PPE in environments where noise is a concern.

Beyond the direct interaction with the laser engraver, other aspects of the workspace require attention to safety. Anti-slip footwear can prevent accidents in environments where materials might fall to the floor or liquids might spill. Furthermore, fire-resistant clothing might be advisable when working with materials that have a high risk of igniting due to the laser's heat.

It's essential for beginners to understand that each laser engraver and material combination may require a specific set of safety equipment. Consulting the laser engraver's manual, material safety data sheets (MSDS) for the materials being engraved, and established safety standards can guide the selection of appropriate PPE. Additionally, attending training sessions or workshops on laser engraver safety can provide hands-on experience and further insights into the necessary precautions.

Employing PPE is just one aspect of a comprehensive safety plan when working with laser engravers. Regular maintenance of the equipment, understanding the operation manuals, and staying informed about the latest safety protocols complement the use of PPE, ensuring a safe and productive environment for laser engraving projects.

For beginners, embracing the full spectrum of safety measures, including the use of appropriate Personal Protective Equipment, not only ensures their protection but also enhances their confidence and efficiency in using laser engravers. Safety, after all, is the foundation upon which creativity and innovation can flourish in the world of laser engraving.

Understanding Laser Classification

Laser classification is an essential aspect of laser engraver safety that every beginner needs to understand before starting their journey into laser engraving. The classification of a laser is determined by its potential for causing damage to human skin or eyes, and understanding these classifications helps users implement the appropriate safety measures when operating a laser engraver.

Lasers are classified into several categories, ranging from Class 1 to Class 4, with each class representing a different level of risk. Class 1 lasers are considered safe under all conditions of normal use, meaning the laser's power is low enough not to cause damage to the eyes or skin. This classification often includes laser printers and CD players, where the laser is fully enclosed during operation, minimizing risk.

Class 2 lasers emit a visible light spectrum, with power not exceeding 1 milliwatt (mW). These are considered low risk because the natural blink reflex of the human eye will typically prevent damage. However, staring into the beam for prolonged periods is not advised. Devices like some laser pointers and barcode scanners fall into this category.

Class 3 lasers are subdivided into Class 3R and Class 3B. Class 3R lasers can be harmful if the beam is directly viewed for extended periods, even though the power does not exceed 5 mW. These require minimal safety measures, such as avoiding direct eye exposure. Class 3B lasers are more hazardous, with a power range between 5 mW and 500 mW. Direct exposure to the beam, even for short periods, can cause serious eye damage, and diffuse reflections may also be harmful. Safety measures for Class 3B lasers include wearing protective eyewear and controlling beam access.

Class 4 lasers are the most dangerous and have a power output of more than 500 mW. They can cause immediate skin burns and eye damage upon direct exposure. Even diffuse reflections of the beam can be hazardous. Class 4 lasers can ignite combustible materials, posing a fire risk. Comprehensive safety measures are mandatory when operating Class 4 lasers, including the use of protective eyewear, strict control of beam access, and training for all users.

For beginners, understanding the class of laser they are working with is crucial for ensuring safety. Most laser engravers used in hobbyist and educational settings are Class 1 or Class 4 machines. Class 1 machines are designed to be safe without additional protective measures, as the laser is contained within an enclosure that prevents exposure during operation. However, many high-powered laser engravers are Class 4 devices, necessitating strict safety protocols to protect the operator and bystanders.

Implementing safety measures for laser engraving involves understanding not only the classification but also the specific risks associated with the laser's operation. This includes knowing the material being engraved, as some materials can emit harmful fumes or particles when engraved. Adequate ventilation or the use of a fume extractor is necessary to mitigate this risk.

Protective eyewear is one of the most critical safety components when working with Class 3B and Class 4 lasers. The eyewear must be specifically designed to filter out the wavelength of the laser, thereby preventing retinal damage. Additionally, ensuring that the work area is restricted and that bystanders are aware of the laser operation is essential for safety.

Understanding laser classification is foundational for anyone beginning to work with laser engravers. It informs the necessary safety protocols, including the use of protective gear and the implementation of safe operational practices. By respecting the power of the laser and adhering to safety guidelines, beginners can safely explore the creative possibilities of laser engraving while protecting themselves and others.

Workspace Setup for Safety

When setting up a workspace for laser engraving, safety should always be the top priority. Laser engravers, while incredibly versatile tools for creating detailed designs on various materials, can also pose significant risks if not used correctly. A well-thought-out workspace not only ensures the safety of the operator but also enhances the efficiency and quality of the engraving process.

Firstly, choosing the right location is crucial. The area should be well-ventilated to prevent the buildup of fumes and particles that can be harmful when inhaled. Many materials, when engraved, emit fumes that can be toxic or irritate the respiratory system. Installing an exhaust fan or an air filtration system can help remove these harmful emissions from the workspace. Additionally, the space should be free from clutter and unnecessary items that could catch fire or obstruct the operation.

Lighting is another critical factor. Adequate lighting reduces the risk of errors and accidents by ensuring that the work area is well-lit and the materials and laser settings can be clearly seen. However, it's important to avoid placing the engraver in direct sunlight as this can interfere with the laser's operation.

The workspace should be equipped with fire safety equipment. Because lasers can generate high temperatures, there's always a risk of fire, especially when working with flammable materials like wood or certain plastics. Having a fire extinguisher readily available and knowing how to use it is essential. Additionally, a bucket of sand or a fire blanket can be useful for smothering fires that may start from the engraving process.

Personal Protective Equipment (PPE) plays a significant role in operator safety. Proper eye protection is a must since the laser beam, or even reflections of it, can cause serious eye injury. Safety glasses designed to block or filter out the laser's wavelength are necessary. It's also wise to wear protective gloves, especially when handling materials that have just been engraved, as they can be hot or have sharp edges.

The laser engraver itself should be placed on a stable, level surface to avoid any unintended movement that could lead to errors or accidents. Ensure that the engraver has enough clearance around it, not just for safety but also to accommodate the size of the materials being engraved.

Electrical safety is paramount. The laser engraver and any associated equipment, like computers or ventilation systems, should be connected to power sources using the correct specifications to prevent electrical fires. Surge protectors and dedicated circuits are recommended to handle the electrical load and protect against potential electrical hazards.

Training and knowledge about the specific laser engraver being used are indispensable for safety. Every operator should read and understand the manufacturer's instructions and safety guidelines. Familiarity with the machine's features, controls, and emergency stop mechanisms is essential before beginning any project.

Establishing rules for the workspace can help maintain a safe environment. This includes protocols for operating the laser engraver, such as never leaving the machine unattended while it's in operation and knowing what materials are safe to engrave. Some materials, like PVC, release chlorine gas when engraved, which can be dangerous to the operator and corrosive to the engraving machine.

Regular maintenance and inspections of the laser engraver are necessary to ensure it remains in good working condition. This includes cleaning the machine, checking for any damaged parts, and ensuring all safety features are functional. A well-maintained machine is less likely to malfunction and pose a safety risk.

Finally, creating a culture of safety within the workspace is vital. This involves continuous learning about laser engraving safety, sharing knowledge among users, and staying updated on best practices and technological advancements in laser engraving.

By meticulously setting up the workspace with safety in mind, operators can minimize risks and focus on the creative possibilities of laser engraving. A safe environment not only protects the operator but also contributes to the overall success and enjoyment of the laser engraving process.

Getting Started with Your Laser Engraver

Unboxing and Setting Up

Embarking on the journey of laser engraving begins with the exhilarating process of unboxing and setting up your new laser engraver, a critical first step that lays the foundation for all your future projects. This stage, filled with anticipation and excitement, is where beginners transform into aspiring engravers, ready to explore the vast potential of their new tool.

The unboxing process starts with carefully removing the laser engraver from its packaging. Manufacturers often secure these machines with foam padding or protective wraps to prevent movement and damage during transportation. As you uncover the engraver, it's important to keep track of all the components. Typically, aside from the main body of the engraver, you'll find an assortment of parts such as the laser tube, power supply, exhaust fan, water pump for cooling (if your model uses a liquid cooling system), and various cables. Some models also include a USB drive with software and manuals, a critical resource for beginners.

Setting up your laser engraver involves several steps, each crucial to ensuring the device operates correctly and safely. First, select an appropriate location for your engraver. This space should be well-ventilated to manage fumes and dust, away from direct sunlight, and stable to prevent any vibrations that could affect the precision of your engravings. Consider the accessibility of power outlets and the space needed for the materials you plan to engrave.

After finding the perfect spot, assemble the laser engraver according to the manufacturer's instructions. This process may vary depending on the model but generally includes installing the laser tube, connecting the exhaust fan, and ensuring the cooling system is properly set up. Pay close attention to the alignment of the laser tube, as this affects the focus and quality of your engravings.

Once the physical setup is complete, the next step is to install the software provided by the manufacturer. This software is essential for creating designs and controlling the laser engraver. Installation is typically straightforward, but refer to the manual for specific instructions. After installing, familiarize yourself with the software's interface and features. Many programs offer a library of preset designs, which is a great starting point for beginners to experiment with.

Connecting your laser engraver to your computer is the final step before you can begin creating. This is usually done via USB or

Ethernet, depending on your model. Once connected, test the connection by sending a simple design to the engraver. This initial test is crucial for ensuring that the software and hardware communicate effectively, and it allows you to troubleshoot any issues before starting on more complex projects.

Before diving into your first project, take the time to understand the safety features of your laser engraver. This includes knowing how to use emergency stops, understanding the signs of malfunction, and familiarizing yourself with the proper maintenance procedures to keep your machine running smoothly.

The process of unboxing and setting up a laser engraver is an adventure filled with learning and discovery. It marks the beginning of a journey where creativity meets technology, opening up a world of possibilities for personal or professional projects. With the setup complete, beginners are now ready to embark on the path of becoming skilled laser engravers, capable of transforming simple materials into works of art.

Understanding Your Laser Engraver's Parts

Getting started with a laser engraver is an exciting journey into the world of precision crafting and design. To harness the full potential of this innovative tool, beginners must first familiarize themselves with its various components. A laser engraver consists of several key parts, each playing a crucial role in the engraving process.

At the heart of the laser engraver is the laser source, which generates the laser beam used for engraving. This component is crucial for determining the power and efficiency of the engraving process. The type of laser—CO2, fiber, or diode—varies depending on the machine and affects the materials it can engrave. CO2 lasers are versatile, ideal for cutting and engraving a wide range of non-metallic materials. Fiber lasers excel with metals and hard plastics, while diode lasers offer a balance suitable for hobbyists working with softer materials and some metals.

The laser beam, once generated, is directed towards the material through a series of mirrors and a focusing lens. The mirrors guide the laser beam in the correct path, while the focusing lens, often adjustable, concentrates the beam to a precise point. This focused laser beam is what burns, cuts, or engraves the material. The ability to adjust the focus is critical, as it allows for control over the depth and precision of the engraving.

The workbed is where the material to be engraved or cut is placed. It's usually adjustable, allowing users to accommodate materials of varying thicknesses. In some laser engravers, the workbed is also capable of moving in the X and Y directions, controlled by stepper motors, which adds to the precision and versatility of the machine. The size of the workbed determines the maximum size of the material that can be worked on, making it an essential consideration for projects.

Controlling the movement of the laser beam and the workbed are the stepper motors, which are connected to a control system. This system, often a computer or a microcontroller, dictates the design to be engraved. Users interface with the control system via software, where they upload or create their designs. This software not only allows for the manipulation and creation of designs but also enables users to adjust settings such as speed, power, and resolution, which are vital for achieving the desired engraving effect.

Safety features are integral to the design of a laser engraver, protecting both the user and the machine. These include safety interlocks that prevent the laser from operating when the cover is open, fume extraction systems to remove harmful byproducts of the engraving process, and cooling systems to prevent overheating. Understanding and maintaining these safety systems is essential for safe and effective operation.

The power supply powers the laser source and the motors, and its capacity is a critical factor in the performance of the laser engraver. Adequate power ensures that the machine can operate at optimal speeds and power settings for various materials.

Lastly, maintenance components such as the laser tube in CO_2 lasers, mirrors, and the lens need regular cleaning and occasional replacement. Keeping these components in good working order ensures the longevity and performance of the laser engraver.

For beginners, understanding these parts and their functions is the first step toward mastering laser engraving. This knowledge not only helps in operating the machine effectively but also in troubleshooting issues, performing maintenance, and ultimately, in creating stunning works of art and design. Whether embarking on a hobby or starting a business, a thorough grasp of the laser engraver's parts is foundational to success in this exciting field.

Initial Machine Calibration

Getting started with a laser engraver is an exciting journey into the world of precision crafting, and one of the first critical steps in this process is the initial machine calibration. This foundational procedure ensures that the laser engraver operates accurately, producing clean, precise cuts and engravings from the very start. Proper calibration sets the stage for the success of all your future projects, ensuring that your creative visions are realized with the highest quality.

When you first set up your laser engraver, it's essential to understand that calibration involves adjusting the machine to work optimally with its environment and the materials you plan to use. This process includes several key steps, each aimed at fine-tuning the machine's performance.

The focal length adjustment is one of the initial calibration tasks. The laser's focal length—the distance between the laser lens and the material surface—needs to be precisely set to focus the laser beam to a fine point. Most machines come with a focusing tool or gauge to help you set this distance accurately. Adjusting the focal length is crucial because it determines the accuracy and quality of the engraving or cut. A perfectly focused laser beam will produce sharp, detailed work, while an improperly focused laser can result in blurry or incomplete engravings.

Aligning the laser beam with the work surface is another essential calibration step. This alignment ensures that the laser hits the material at the correct angle and position, which is particularly important for achieving uniform engraving depths and clean cuts. In some machines, this might involve manually adjusting mirrors or lenses to direct the beam accurately. Test engravings on scrap material can help you gauge the alignment and make necessary adjustments.

Software calibration is also a vital part of the setup process. This involves configuring the software that controls the laser engraver to match the specifics of your machine and material. Parameters such as power, speed, and pulse rate need to be adjusted according to the material you're working with. Different materials absorb and reflect the laser beam differently, so calibrating these settings ensures that the laser engraves or cuts efficiently without damaging the material.

Calibrating for material thickness is an important step that is often overlooked. The laser must be set to account for the height of the material you are using. Many laser engravers have an adjustable bed or a z-axis that can be moved up or down. Calibrating the machine to the specific thickness of the material ensures that the focal length remains correct throughout the engraving or cutting process.

Finally, performing a test run is an indispensable part of the calibration process. Once all adjustments have been made, running a test engraving or cut on a piece of scrap material of the same type as your project material allows you to see the actual results of your calibration efforts. This step not only helps in fine-tuning the settings but also provides a practical understanding of how changes in calibration affect the outcome. Observing the results, you might need to go back and readjust certain settings, learning through trial and error what works best for your specific machine and project needs.

Initial machine calibration might seem like a time-consuming and meticulous process, especially for beginners, but it is a crucial investment in the quality of your future projects. Taking the time to properly calibrate your laser engraver pays off in the long run by minimizing errors, reducing material waste, and ensuring that your creative projects are executed with precision and excellence. As you grow more familiar with your machine and the calibration process, these initial steps become second nature, paving the way for endless possibilities in laser engraving and cutting.

Choosing the Right Material for Your Project

Choosing the right material for your laser engraving project is a pivotal decision that significantly affects the outcome and quality of your work. Each material interacts with the laser beam differently, influencing not only the aesthetic appeal of the final product but also its functionality and durability. This decision becomes even more critical for beginners, who are still navigating the complexities of laser engraving. Understanding the properties, advantages, and limitations of various materials is essential for achieving the desired results and maximizing the potential of your laser engraver.

Wood is among the most popular materials for laser engraving, cherished for its natural beauty and the depth it adds to engraved designs. Different types of wood, including maple, cherry, and walnut, offer varying degrees of hardness, which affects how the laser cuts or engraves the material. Softer woods tend to engrave deeper and faster but might burn more easily, while harder woods require more power and slower speeds for a clear engraving. The choice of wood impacts the contrast and clarity of the engraved design, making it a versatile option for both beginners and experienced users.

Acrylic, available in cast and extruded forms, is another favorite for laser engravers. Cast acrylic is preferred for engraving, as it produces a frosty, white contrast against the clear material, ideal for awards and signs. Extruded acrylic, while better suited for cutting, tends to leave a clear engraving that lacks contrast. Acrylic's ability to be cut and engraved with precision makes it perfect for detailed projects requiring a sleek, modern finish.

Metals require a specific approach since direct laser engraving is typically limited to coated metals or those treated with a marking compound. The laser removes the coating or reacts with the marking compound to create a permanent mark on the metal surface. This method is widely used for industrial tags, personalized jewelry, and decorative items. Direct engraving on metals like stainless steel and aluminum often requires a fiber laser, which may not be available to beginners. However, coated metals and metal sheets designed for laser engraving offer a practical alternative.

Glass engraving with a laser offers a unique aesthetic but can be challenging due to the material's fragility and the potential for inconsistent results. The laser tends to fracture the surface of the glass, creating a frosted appearance that can vary depending on the type of glass and the settings used. Experimenting with power and speed settings is crucial to minimize cracks and achieve a smooth finish.

Glass is ideal for decorative items, awards, and personalized gifts, where a delicate and elegant appearance is desired.

Leather and faux leather are excellent materials for laser engraving, offering a rich, sophisticated look. Genuine leather varies in its reaction to laser engraving, with different types and treatments affecting the outcome. It's important to test small samples to determine the optimal settings for the desired effect. Faux leather provides a more consistent surface for engraving, making it a good starting point for those new to working with leather materials.

Paper and cardboard are perhaps the most accessible materials for laser engraving, perfect for invitations, business cards, and prototypes. These materials can be engraved and cut with high precision, allowing for intricate designs and delicate cut-outs. The key is to use low power and high speed to prevent burning, making paper and cardboard ideal for beginners looking to practice their designs before moving on to more challenging materials.

Fabric and textiles open up a world of possibilities for laser engraving, from personalized apparel to unique home décor. Natural fibers like cotton, silk, and denim respond well to laser engraving, which can etch detailed designs without fraying the material. Synthetic fabrics require careful handling, as they can melt or distort under the laser. Testing is essential to ensure the laser settings yield the desired effect without damaging the fabric.

Choosing the right material for your laser engraving project involves considering the material's properties, the intended use of the finished product, and your level of experience with the laser engraver. Experimentation and practice are key to understanding how different materials react to the laser, enabling beginners to make informed decisions and achieve successful outcomes in their projects. Whether you're creating a personalized gift, a prototype, or a piece of art, the choice of material plays a crucial role in bringing your vision to life with laser engraving.

Software and Design Basics

Choosing the Right Software

Selecting the appropriate software is a pivotal step in mastering laser engraving, especially for beginners. The software acts as a bridge between your creative ideas and the physical world, translating your designs into precise instructions for the laser engraver. With a myriad of options available, understanding the key features to look for can significantly impact the quality and ease of your engraving projects.

First and foremost, compatibility with your laser engraver is essential. Ensure the software you choose can communicate effectively with your machine. Most engravers come with recommended software, but exploring third-party options can offer enhanced functionality. Check for supported file formats, as you'll want the flexibility to import various types of design files, such as SVG, DXF, JPG, or PNG, depending on your project needs.

Ease of use is another crucial factor. Beginners should look for software with an intuitive interface, straightforward navigation, and comprehensive tutorials or support resources. The learning curve associated with new software can be steep, so access to online forums, instructional videos, and customer support can be invaluable resources as you get acquainted with the program.

Look for software that offers a robust set of design and editing tools. Even if you plan to create most of your designs in another program, having the ability to make last-minute adjustments or enhancements directly in the engraving software is highly beneficial. Features like text addition, shape manipulation, and image tracing can save time and expand your creative possibilities.

The precision of your engravings is largely dependent on the software's ability to finely control the laser. Look for software that allows you to adjust settings such as power, speed, and resolution. These controls will enable you to tailor the engraving process to different materials and design intricacies, resulting in higher quality finishes and reducing the risk of errors.

Advanced features, such as the ability to simulate your final engraving, can be extremely helpful. This allows you to preview how your design will appear on the material, helping to avoid costly mistakes and material wastage. While not essential for beginners, features like 3D engraving capabilities, color mapping, and layer management can become increasingly valuable as your skills progress.

Consider the software's update and upgrade policies. Regular updates are important for maintaining compatibility with operating systems and for accessing improved features and bug fixes. Some software offers a one-time purchase, while others operate on a subscription model. Evaluate which financial model aligns with your usage expectations and budget.

Lastly, the community and ecosystem surrounding the software can offer additional benefits. A vibrant user community not only provides support and inspiration but also a wealth of shared resources, such as templates and tutorials. Software developers that encourage user feedback and actively engage with their community are often quicker to innovate and respond to user needs.

Choosing the right software for laser engraving involves a careful balance of compatibility, ease of use, design capabilities, precision control, and community support. Beginners should prioritize user-friendly interfaces and comprehensive learning resources to ease the initial learning phase. As skills and confidence grow, more advanced features and customization options will become increasingly important. Selecting software that grows with you can transform your laser engraving journey from a tentative first step to a landscape of limitless creative exploration.

Designing for Laser Engraving: Tips and Tricks

Designing for laser engraving presents a unique set of challenges and opportunities. The process converts digital artwork into physical pieces, and understanding the nuances of both software and material interaction is key. For beginners venturing into the world of laser engraving, mastering the design phase is crucial for achieving outstanding results.

Selecting the right software is the first step in this journey. Vector-based programs like Adobe Illustrator or Inkscape are popular choices because they allow for precise control over design elements. These programs enable users to create designs that are scalable without losing quality, which is essential for detailed engraving work. For those looking to engrave photographs or complex images, raster-based software like Adobe Photoshop can be used to edit images to enhance contrast and detail, which improves the engraving quality.

Understanding the material you intend to engrave on is just as important as the design itself. Different materials react in unique ways to the laser's heat. For example, wood offers a natural and warm look but requires adjustments in speed and power to avoid burning. Acrylic, on the other hand, can produce a very clean and precise engraving but might require multiple passes for depth. Experimentation is key; starting with low power and increasing gradually can help determine the optimal settings for each material.

When designing, consider the contrast and legibility of your artwork. High contrast designs tend to yield the best results because the laser engraver essentially works in a binary mode, engraving or not engraving. Utilizing bold lines and avoiding fine, intricate details can enhance readability, especially on smaller objects. However, when fine detail is necessary, ensure the resolution of your design matches the capabilities of your laser engraver to avoid losing detail in the engraving process.

Line weight plays a significant role in the outcome of your engraved design. Thicker lines are more forgiving and can produce a more pronounced effect, while thinner lines can be elegant but may risk being too faint if the engraver's settings aren't precisely tuned. It's beneficial to create a design guide or template with varying line weights and patterns to test on your chosen material, which can serve as a reference for future projects.

Spacing and layout considerations are crucial, especially when working with text or combined elements. Ensure there is adequate spacing between characters and design elements to prevent them from blending together during the engraving process. This is particularly important when working with materials that have a tendency to burn or melt slightly, such as wood or certain plastics.

Incorporating negative space into your design can produce striking effects, especially on materials that contrast sharply when engraved, such as coated metals or colored acrylics. This technique can add depth and dimension to your work, making the engraved elements stand out more prominently.

Testing is an indispensable part of the design process. Before committing to the final piece, engrave your design on a sample piece of your chosen material. This allows you to adjust the design, software settings, and laser parameters as needed. Keeping a log of these tests, including power, speed, frequency, and material, can be a valuable resource for refining your technique and achieving consistent results.

Finally, remember that laser engraving is as much an art as it is a science. Each project offers a chance to learn and improve. Embrace the learning curve, and don't be afraid to experiment with different designs, materials, and techniques. With patience and practice, you'll develop a keen sense of how to best translate your digital designs into beautifully engraved creations, making each project a unique reflection of your artistic vision and technical skill.

Preparing Your Design for Engraving

When embarking on the journey of laser engraving, the preparation of your design is a critical step that bridges the gap between a creative idea and its tangible realization. This process involves selecting the right software, understanding design basics, and fine-tuning your artwork to ensure it is perfectly suited for the laser engraving process.

Choosing the right software is the first crucial step. Most laser engravers come with proprietary software, but there are several other options available that might offer a more intuitive interface or additional features. Software like Adobe Illustrator, CorelDRAW, and Inkscape are popular choices for their flexibility and comprehensive toolsets. These programs allow you to create vector graphics, which are ideal for laser engraving due to their scalability and precision. Vector files define shapes using mathematical equations, ensuring that your design remains crisp and clear regardless of size adjustments, a critical aspect when working with various materials and engraving sizes.

Understanding the basics of design within these programs can significantly impact the quality of your final engraved piece. Key principles such as contrast, balance, and simplicity play vital roles. For laser engraving, designs with high contrast between elements tend to yield the best results, as the laser can better differentiate between areas to be engraved and those to be left untouched. Balancing intricate details with simpler elements ensures that your design is legible and effective, especially on smaller objects where too much detail can lead to a cluttered and indiscernible outcome.

Simplicity in your design not only aids in the clarity of the final engraved product but also in the engraving process itself. Complex designs with numerous small details may look stunning on screen but can become problematic when translated into a physical engraving, leading to longer engraving times and potential errors. It's beneficial to simplify your design to its most impactful elements, ensuring that it communicates your intended message or aesthetic without overwhelming the material it's engraved on.

Once your design is complete, converting it into a format compatible with your laser engraver is essential. This usually means saving your artwork as a vector file, such as an SVG, EPS, or AI format, although some engravers may require different or specific file types. It's also important to consider the color mode of your design; most laser engraving processes interpret colors as different engraving depths or speeds, so adjusting your design to a grayscale palette can help in visualizing and controlling the outcome.

Preparing your design for engraving also involves understanding the material you plan to use. Different materials react differently to the laser's power and speed, and your design may need to be adjusted accordingly. For example, engraving on wood requires considering the wood's grain, which can affect the uniformity and clarity of the engraving. Testing your design on a sample piece of your chosen material can provide valuable insights into how your settings affect the final result and allow you to make necessary adjustments before proceeding with the final piece.

Finally, the alignment and positioning of your design within the engraving area are crucial for achieving the desired outcome. Ensure that your design is centered or appropriately placed according to your vision, taking into account the dimensions of the material you're working with. Most engraving software offers tools for precisely positioning your design, which is particularly useful when working on projects that require exact alignment, such as engraving multiple pieces with the same design.

By carefully selecting the appropriate software, understanding design principles, simplifying your artwork, and adjusting for material specifics, you can prepare your design for laser engraving with confidence. This meticulous preparation not only ensures that your creative vision is realized but also optimizes the engraving process, leading to high-quality, impactful results that truly showcase the potential of laser engraving.

Testing Your Design on Different Materials

Testing your design on different materials is a pivotal step in mastering laser engraving, as it directly impacts the final outcome of your project. Different materials react uniquely to the laser engraving process, making experimentation and adjustment essential for achieving the desired results. Understanding the nuances of how various materials interact with laser engraving can transform a beginner into a skilled artisan.

When starting with laser engraving, most beginners experiment with wood due to its forgiving nature and the beautiful contrast that can be achieved. However, the type of wood plays a significant role in the outcome. Softwoods like pine engrave quickly due to their lower density but can result in uneven textures. Hardwoods like maple or cherry offer a smoother finish but require more power or slower speeds. Testing your design on scraps of the intended wood type allows you to adjust the laser's power and speed settings, ensuring a clean and precise engraving.

Acrylic is another popular material, offering two distinct finishes depending on its type. Cast acrylic when engraved produces a frosty white contrast that is excellent for signage or awards, while extruded acrylic tends to be clearer and less distinct. The key to engraving acrylic lies in finding the right balance of speed and power, ensuring the edges of your design are crisp and the surface isn't overheated.

Metal engraving with a laser engraver usually requires a special marking compound for hobbyist machines, as these lasers can't engrave metal directly. Testing on metal involves applying the compound evenly, letting it dry, and then engraving. The process can be finicky, and finding the right settings is crucial to avoid burning the compound or failing to mark the metal entirely. Practicing on similar metals helps refine the process before moving on to the final piece.

Glass offers a unique challenge due to its fragile nature and the risk of cracking under the heat of the laser. Low power settings and high speeds are a good starting point, with testing focusing on achieving a smooth, frosted appearance without causing fractures. Experimentation is key, as factors like glass thickness and composition can significantly affect the outcome.

Leather, whether genuine or synthetic, provides a rich, luxurious medium for laser engraving, but it requires careful handling. The laser can easily burn leather, so testing helps determine the lowest possible power setting that still achieves a clear, visible engraving. Each type of leather reacts differently, making it essential to test on offcuts of the same material to fine-tune the settings.

Rubber, used for making stamps and other flexible items, absorbs the laser energy efficiently, meaning lower power settings are usually sufficient. However, the density of the rubber can vary, affecting the depth and clarity of the engraving. Testing on a similar rubber piece helps avoid melting or warping the material.

Paper and cardboard are perhaps the most delicate materials to work with. They require very low power settings and fast speeds to prevent burning. Testing on these materials allows you to achieve the fine balance necessary for detailed engravings without igniting the paper.

For each material, the process of testing involves starting with the manufacturer's recommended settings as a baseline and then adjusting based on the results. Keeping a detailed log of these tests, including material type, laser settings, and outcomes, becomes an invaluable resource for future projects. This iterative process not only improves the quality of your engravings but also deepens your understanding of how laser engraving interacts with different materials.

Software plays a crucial role in this testing phase. Most laser engraving software allows for the simulation of the engraving process, providing a preliminary visual of how the design might look on the material. However, there's no substitute for physical testing. The software's ability to adjust power, speed, and frequency settings in response to test results is critical, enabling fine-tuning that aligns with the material's characteristics.

Testing your design on different materials is an essential step in the laser engraving process, offering a hands-on learning experience that refines both your technical skills and artistic vision. Through careful experimentation and adjustment, beginners can navigate the challenges presented by each material, leading to successful and satisfying engraving projects.

Operating Your Laser Engraver

Step-by-Step Guide to Your First Engraving

Embarking on the journey of your first laser engraving project can be an exciting yet daunting task. With the right guidance, however, you'll find yourself creating stunning pieces in no time. This guide is tailored for beginners, taking you through each step of operating your laser engraver, ensuring your initial venture into laser engraving is both successful and enjoyable.

Start by selecting the right material for your project. Different materials react uniquely to the laser's heat, so it's crucial to choose one that aligns with your project's needs and the capabilities of your machine. Popular options include wood, acrylic, and leather, each offering its own aesthetic and textural qualities. Ensure the material is clean, flat, and free from any coatings that might interfere with the engraving process.

Next, prepare your design using the appropriate software. Most laser engravers come with their own software or are compatible with common graphic design programs. For your first project, start with a simple design to understand how the software translates your design onto the material. Keep in mind the dimensions of your material and adjust your design accordingly. Once satisfied, save your design in the format recommended by your laser engraver's manual.

Before you start engraving, make sure your laser engraver is set up correctly. This includes checking that the laser is focused properly, the ventilation is adequate, and all safety measures are in place. Focusing the laser is critical as it affects the quality of the engraving. Follow your machine's instructions to adjust the focus until it's optimized for your material's thickness.

Now, position your material on the engraving platform. The placement is vital for ensuring the design is engraved where you want it on the material. Use rulers or jigs if necessary to align your material precisely. Many laser engravers feature red dot pointers or other alignment tools to assist in this process.

With your material in place, it's time to set the engraving parameters. This includes the power, speed, and resolution settings of the laser. The correct settings depend on the material you're using and the complexity of your design. A general rule is to use higher speed and lower power for lighter engraving and slower speed and higher power for deeper cuts. Your laser engraver's manual should provide guidelines for these settings based on different materials.

Once everything is set up, perform a final check to ensure the laser path is clear, and the ventilation system is functioning correctly. It's also a good idea to do a test run on a scrap piece of material if available. This helps you see how your settings affect the material and allows you to make any necessary adjustments before proceeding with the final piece.

Now, you're ready to begin the engraving process. Start the laser engraver according to the manufacturer's instructions. Stay present during the engraving process to monitor progress and to be able to quickly intervene in case of an error or malfunction. Watching your design come to life is one of the most rewarding aspects of laser engraving.

After the engraving is complete, allow the material and machine to cool down if necessary before removing the finished piece. Clean your engraved piece following the recommended practices for your material, removing any residue or debris from the engraving process.

Finally, inspect your work. Take note of any areas where the engraving might not have come out as expected and consider what adjustments can be made in future projects to improve. Every project is a learning opportunity, and with practice, you'll refine your technique and be able to tackle more complex designs and materials.

Material Placement and Focus Adjustment

Mastering material placement and focus adjustment is crucial when operating a laser engraver, especially for beginners looking to achieve precision and quality in their projects. These two aspects are foundational to the laser engraving process, affecting the accuracy, depth, and overall quality of the engraving.

Material placement is the first step in preparing for laser engraving. The material must be positioned correctly on the engraving bed to ensure that the design is engraved in the desired location and orientation. It's important to secure the material to prevent any movement during the engraving process, as even slight shifts can lead to misalignment and unsatisfactory results. Various methods can be used to secure materials, including the use of honeycomb beds, magnetic mats, or even simple tape for lighter materials. For materials with irregular shapes or sizes, custom jigs can be created to hold them in place, ensuring consistent placement for multiple engraving runs.

Once the material is properly positioned, the next critical step is adjusting the focus of the laser. The focus determines the laser beam's precision at the point of contact with the material. When the laser is perfectly focused, it produces a sharp and efficient cut or engrave. If the laser is out of focus, the energy is spread over a larger area, resulting in weaker engraving strength, less detail, and potentially uneven depths. Most laser engravers come with a focusing tool or gauge to help adjust the distance between the laser and the material's surface. This distance varies depending on the type of laser and the material being used but is typically in the range of a few millimeters.

For beginners, understanding how to adjust the focus is essential. The process usually involves loosening a focus ring or lever, moving the laser head up or down until the correct focus distance is achieved, and then tightening it back into place. Some modern laser engravers feature automatic focusing capabilities, which can greatly simplify the process, although it's still important for users to understand how focus affects the engraving.

The focus can also be adjusted creatively to produce different engraving effects. For example, defocusing the laser slightly can create a broader engraving line, which can be desirable for certain designs or effects. Experimenting with different focus settings on scrap material is a good practice for beginners to see firsthand how focus adjustments impact the final result.

Understanding the properties of the material being engraved is also crucial when adjusting focus. Different materials absorb and reflect laser light differently, and their thickness and density can affect the optimal focus distance. For instance, softer materials like wood might require a different focus setting than harder materials like acrylic or metal. Additionally, if engraving on a curved or uneven surface, the focus may need to be adjusted during the engraving process to accommodate changes in material height.

Accurate material placement and focus adjustment are skills that improve with practice. Beginners are encouraged to start with simpler projects on more forgiving materials, gradually moving on to more complex designs and materials as they become more comfortable with the process. Keeping a log of successful settings for different materials and designs can also be helpful, providing a reference for future projects and reducing the trial-and-error process.

In conclusion, mastering material placement and focus adjustment is fundamental for anyone starting with laser engraving. These steps directly impact the quality and precision of the engraving, making them critical skills to develop. Through practice, experimentation, and a careful understanding of their laser engraver's capabilities, beginners can achieve professional-level results and bring their creative visions to life.

Configuring Power, Speed, and Resolution

Configuring power, speed, and resolution are critical steps in the operation of a laser engraver, directly impacting the quality, efficiency, and outcome of the engraving process. Beginners must understand the interplay between these settings to achieve optimal results on various materials and for different design complexities.

Power refers to the intensity of the laser beam, measured in watts. Adjusting the power is essential for controlling the depth and darkness of the engraving. High power settings are suitable for engraving harder materials like metal or for achieving deeper cuts in wood or acrylic. However, too much power can lead to burning or excessive material removal. On softer materials like paper or thin fabrics, lower power settings are recommended to prevent damage. Finding the right balance requires experimentation and familiarity with the material's reaction to the laser.

Speed, on the other hand, determines how fast the laser moves over the material's surface. High-speed settings are efficient for quick surface markings or when working with heat-sensitive materials, as they minimize the risk of burning or warping. However, too high a speed might result in shallow or uneven engravings. Lower speeds allow for deeper cuts and are ideal for materials that can withstand prolonged exposure to the laser without degrading. The correct speed setting depends on the desired engraving depth and the material's heat tolerance.

Resolution, expressed in dots per inch (DPI), affects the engraving's detail level. High-resolution settings produce finer details, making them ideal for intricate designs or small text. This setting is crucial for achieving clear, precise outcomes, especially on materials like metal, where detail work is highly valued. Lower resolutions are faster and more suitable for larger designs or when detail is less critical. Balancing resolution with speed and power is key to efficient and effective engraving, as high-resolution engravings require slower speeds or higher power to maintain clarity.

The interplay between power, speed, and resolution is material-dependent. Hard materials like metal and glass typically require high power and low speed to etch effectively. Conversely, softer materials like wood and leather may need lower power settings or higher speeds to avoid burning. The resolution is adjusted based on the complexity of the design and the engraving's purpose.

Experimentation plays a crucial role in mastering these settings. Beginners are encouraged to start with manufacturer-recommended settings for various materials and then adjust based on the specific needs of their project. Creating a reference chart or log of successful settings for different materials and designs can serve as a valuable tool for future projects.

Understanding the effects of power, speed, and resolution adjustments also involves recognizing signs of improper settings. Excessive burning, incomplete cuts, or faint engravings indicate the need for setting adjustments. Learning to read the material's response to the laser allows for real-time changes and ultimately leads to mastering the art of laser engraving.

Configuring power, speed, and resolution is foundational to operating a laser engraver effectively. Beginners should approach these settings as tools for creativity and precision, understanding that mastery comes with experimentation, practice, and patience. As they gain experience, users will develop an intuitive sense of how to adjust these parameters to achieve their desired results, whether working on personal projects or commercial products. This knowledge not only enhances the quality of the engravings but also expands the range of materials and designs that can be successfully executed.

Troubleshooting Common Issues

When operating a laser engraver, beginners might encounter various issues that can affect the quality of their projects or even halt their progress. Understanding how to troubleshoot these common problems is crucial for maintaining a smooth workflow and achieving the desired results.

One frequent issue is the laser not firing, which could be due to several factors, such as incorrect settings, a malfunctioning laser tube, or electrical problems. First, ensure that the power settings are correctly adjusted for the material being engraved. If the settings are correct but the laser still isn't firing, inspect the laser tube for any visible damage or signs of wear. It's also wise to check the electrical connections to make sure everything is securely connected and there are no loose wires.

Another common challenge is the laser engraving appearing faint or uneven. This can often be traced back to incorrect focus or inappropriate power and speed settings. To resolve this, adjust the focus of the laser to match the thickness of the material. Experiment with different power and speed settings on a sample piece to find the optimal balance for your specific material. Remember, too much power can burn the material, while too little power might not engrave it at all.

Sometimes, the engraved design might be misaligned or not where it was expected to be. This issue usually stems from improper calibration of the laser engraver or inaccuracies in the design software settings. Recalibrating the machine according to the manufacturer's instructions can often fix this problem. Additionally, double-check the alignment settings in your design software to ensure they match the actual layout of the material on the engraving bed.

Uneven engraving depth across a project is another issue that operators might face. This problem can arise from an uneven engraving bed or material that is not perfectly flat. To counteract this, ensure that the engraving bed is level and that the material is securely fastened down. Using a reliable material holding system can prevent shifting or warping during the engraving process.

Experiencing a reduction in engraving quality over time is not uncommon and can be due to a dirty lens or mirrors. The buildup of debris from the engraving process can interfere with the laser's ability to focus correctly. Cleaning the lens and mirrors regularly with a proper cleaning solution and a soft, lint-free cloth can restore the clarity and precision of the laser beam.

Another issue is the appearance of burn marks on the material, especially when working with wood or other flammable materials.

Reducing the laser's power or increasing its speed can help minimize burning. Additionally, using a protective covering like masking tape over the engraving area can reduce surface burn marks and can be easily removed after the engraving process.

Lastly, software-related issues can also hinder the operation of a laser engraver. Compatibility problems between the engraving software and the computer's operating system can cause errors or prevent the software from functioning correctly. Ensure that your software is up to date and compatible with your operating system. If problems persist, consulting the software's customer support or online forums can provide solutions specific to your software version and operating system.

Troubleshooting these common issues requires patience and a methodical approach. By understanding the potential problems that can arise when operating a laser engraver and knowing how to address them, beginners can enhance their skills and confidence in using this powerful tool. Regular maintenance, proper calibration, and a willingness to experiment with settings are key factors in overcoming these challenges and achieving consistent, high-quality engraving results.

Advanced Techniques and Tips

Engraving Different Materials (Wood, Acrylic, Metal, Glass)

Laser engraving different materials requires understanding their unique properties and how they interact with laser technology. This knowledge allows for the adaptation of techniques to achieve optimal results, whether working with wood, acrylic, metal, or glass. Each material offers distinct challenges and rewards, making versatility a key skill in mastering laser engraving.

Wood is one of the most popular materials for laser engraving due to its natural beauty and the depth of contrast that can be achieved. Softwoods like pine and cedar engrave with less power and faster speeds, ideal for beginners looking to practice and refine their skills. Hardwoods, such as oak and maple, require more power but can produce exceptionally detailed and rich engravings. When engraving wood, it's crucial to consider the direction of the grain; engraving along the grain can yield different textures and visual effects. An advanced tip for wood engraving is to use masking tape over the engraving area to reduce charring and achieve a cleaner finish, which is especially useful for intricate designs.

Acrylic, both clear and colored, offers a smooth surface that responds well to laser engraving, producing a frosted appearance that contrasts beautifully against the glossy finish of the material. To achieve the best results with acrylic, using a lower power setting and a high speed helps prevent melting or warping. Reverse engraving on the backside of clear acrylic can create a visually striking depth effect, enhancing the three-dimensionality of the design. Experimenting with different types of acrylic can also yield various effects, such as mirrored or fluorescent finishes, providing a broad canvas for creative expression.

Metal engraving with a laser requires a different approach, as most lasers cannot directly engrave metal surfaces without assistance. Coated metals, anodized aluminum, or specially treated metals designed for laser engraving are the exceptions. For other types of metal, a marking compound can be applied to the surface before engraving, which the laser then fuses to the metal, creating a permanent mark. Precision is key when engraving metal, as the material's durability leaves little room for error. Post-engraving, cleaning the metal to remove any residue from the marking compound reveals the engraved design in stunning clarity and detail.

Glass engraving with a laser produces a delicate, frosted effect that is highly sought after for decorative items, awards, and personalized gifts. However, glass is prone to cracking or chipping under the laser's heat.

To mitigate this, applying a thin layer of dish soap or using a low power setting can help evenly distribute the heat, reducing the risk of damage. Another technique involves experimenting with defocusing the laser slightly, which spreads the beam over a larger area, softening the impact on the glass surface. This method can be particularly effective for achieving a smooth, uniform engraving on glassware or windows.

Across all materials, mastering the art of laser engraving involves a delicate balance between power, speed, and focus. Understanding the nuances of each material—not just in terms of how it engraves but also in how it reacts to the heat and energy of the laser—is crucial. Beginners are encouraged to start with simple projects and materials that are more forgiving, gradually working their way up to more complex compositions and challenging materials. Keeping a detailed log of settings used for different materials and designs can serve as a valuable reference, helping to replicate success and learn from past attempts.

Experimentation plays a significant role in mastering laser engraving, as does patience and a willingness to learn from mistakes. Each material offers a unique canvas for creativity, and with practice, even beginners can achieve professional-grade engravings that elevate their projects to new levels of craftsmanship and artistry.

Multi-Layered Engraving

Multi-layered engraving is a sophisticated technique that elevates the art of laser engraving to new heights of complexity and beauty. By etching designs across multiple layers or depths within a single material, artisans can create stunning visual effects, adding dimensionality and texture to their work. This approach not only enhances the aesthetic appeal of engraved items but also allows for a greater expression of creativity and precision in design execution.

To embark on multi-layered engraving, understanding the capabilities and settings of your laser engraver is paramount. This process involves adjusting the laser's power, speed, and focus to vary the depth and intensity of the engraving with each pass. The goal is to carefully control these variables to achieve the desired contrast and depth without compromising the integrity of the material. Beginners should start by experimenting with these settings on scrap material, noting how changes affect the outcome, to develop a feel for how their specific machine interacts with different materials.

The choice of material plays a crucial role in the success of multi-layered engraving. Materials that can withstand multiple passes of the laser without degrading are ideal. Wood, with its natural layers and varying densities, is particularly suited to this technique, as it allows for subtle gradations in depth and tone. Acrylics and certain metals can also be used effectively, offering a different but equally captivating aesthetic. It's important to select materials that do not burn or melt easily under repeated laser exposure, as the precision required for multi-layered engraving demands several passes over the same area.

Design preparation is another critical aspect. Designs intended for multi-layered engraving should be created with layers in mind, using shading or varying line weights to indicate different depths. Software capable of handling complex designs and translating them into instructions for the laser engraver is essential. Many modern laser engravers come with or are compatible with sophisticated software that allows for intricate control over the engraving process. Understanding how to use this software to its full potential is key to achieving successful multi-layered engravings.

Executing a multi-layered engraving requires patience and precision. The process generally involves making several passes with the laser, each at a different setting, to gradually build up the layers of the design. It's essential to monitor the progress carefully, adjusting settings as needed based on the material's response to the engraving. For example, if the material is wood, you may need to lower the power or increase the speed on softer areas to prevent burning or over-engraving.

Aftercare of multi-layered engravings is just as important as the engraving process itself. Depending on the material, finishing touches might include cleaning, sanding, or applying a sealant to protect the engraved surfaces and enhance their visual depth. This final step is crucial in bringing out the contrast and detail in the layers, transforming the piece from a simple engraved item into a work of art.

For those looking to explore the full potential of their laser engraver, multi-layered engraving offers a challenging but rewarding avenue. With practice, beginners can master this advanced technique, unlocking new possibilities for creativity and innovation in their laser engraving projects. The key to success lies in understanding your machine's capabilities, choosing the right materials, preparing intricate designs, and executing with care and precision. As skills develop, so too will the complexity and beauty of the engravings produced, making multi-layered engraving a technique well worth mastering for any aspiring laser engraver.

Using Jigs for Batch Production

Using jigs for batch production in laser engraving is a game-changer for those looking to streamline their workflow and increase efficiency. A jig, essentially a custom-made template, holds the workpieces in place during the engraving process, ensuring consistency and precision across multiple items. This technique is particularly valuable for beginners who have moved past single-piece projects and are looking to undertake larger orders or create multiple copies of a design.

When embarking on batch production, the first step is designing the jig. This involves creating a template that fits the laser engraver's work area and has cut-outs or holders tailored to the specific dimensions of the items being engraved. For instance, if you're engraving multiple wooden coasters, the jig would have circular cut-outs matching the coasters' diameter, ensuring each piece is positioned correctly under the laser.

Material choice for the jig is crucial. Most users opt for materials that are durable yet easy to cut with a laser, such as thin plywood or acrylic. The key is to select a material that won't degrade quickly after repeated use but is also not so thick that it significantly reduces the laser's work area.

Creating the jig itself can be a meticulous process. Precision in the design phase ensures that the cut-outs or holders perfectly match the dimensions of the items to be engraved. Utilizing software that accompanies the laser engraver, you can draw the layout of the jig, including all necessary cut-outs. Once the design is finalized, the laser is used to cut the jig out of the chosen material, creating a reusable template for batch production.

One of the major advantages of using jigs is the significant reduction in setup time for each engraving session. Once the jig is placed in the laser engraver, multiple items can be engraved in rapid succession, with minimal intervention required between pieces. This not only speeds up the production process but also minimizes the risk of human error, leading to a uniform finish on each piece.

Another benefit is the ability to maximize the use of available space on the laser bed. By designing jigs that hold items close together, you can engrave more pieces in a single run, making efficient use of both time and materials. This spatial efficiency is particularly important for users with smaller laser engravers, where work area is at a premium.

Jigs also open the door to personalization within batch production. For example, if creating a set of personalized wooden pens, a jig can hold each pen in place while the laser engraves names or messages on them.

Even though each piece might have a different engraving, the jig ensures that the positioning is consistent across the batch.

Maintaining the jig and laser engraver is essential for long-term success. Over time, residue from the engraving process can accumulate on the jig, affecting its precision. Regular cleaning and inspections ensure that the jig continues to position items accurately. Similarly, keeping the laser engraver in good working condition, with regular maintenance of its components, ensures that it continues to interact with the jig effectively, producing high-quality engravings every time.

For beginners looking to venture into batch production with laser engraving, mastering the use of jigs is a pivotal skill. It not only boosts productivity but also elevates the quality of the finished products, paving the way for taking on larger projects or starting a laser engraving business. By investing time in designing and creating effective jigs, users can transform their approach to laser engraving, moving from crafting individual pieces to producing high-quality work in volume.

Tips for Improving Engraving Quality

Mastering the art of laser engraving requires more than just understanding the basics; it demands a keen eye for detail and a willingness to explore advanced techniques that can significantly enhance the quality of your engravings. For beginners ready to elevate their craft, several tips can help refine their skills and produce superior results.

One of the first steps to improving engraving quality is selecting the right materials. Each material reacts differently to the laser's heat, so choosing materials that are known for their engraving quality, such as certain types of wood, acrylic, and anodized aluminum, can make a big difference. Experimenting with different materials and documenting the results helps in understanding how to adjust settings for optimal outcomes.

Proper preparation of the material is just as important as the material selection itself. Cleaning the surface to remove dust, oils, and residues ensures that the laser can work efficiently, resulting in cleaner and more precise engravings. Applying a masking tape over the engraving area can also reduce residue from the engraving process and enhance the contrast of the final product.

Adjusting the laser's speed and power settings is crucial for achieving the best engraving quality. Lower speed settings allow the laser more time to burn the material, which can be useful for darker and deeper engraves, but there's a fine balance as too low of a speed can lead to burning or excessive charring. Experimenting with different combinations of speed and power settings on scrap material before starting on the final piece can save time and resources in the long run.

Focusing the laser precisely is another critical factor. An improperly focused laser can result in blurry engravings with poor detail. Most laser engravers come with focusing tools or procedures to ensure the laser is at the optimal distance from the material. Regular checks and adjustments ensure consistent engraving quality across different projects.

The use of air assist, which blows a stream of air at the point of contact between the laser and the material, can greatly improve the quality of the engraving. The air helps to remove debris and prevent flaming, thus avoiding burn marks on the material. It also keeps the lens cleaner for longer, providing consistent results.

Grayscale graphics and dithering techniques can add depth and texture to laser engravings, creating more dynamic and visually appealing pieces. Learning how to effectively use these techniques requires practice and experimentation but can set your work apart from the rest.

Regular maintenance of the laser engraver is essential for ensuring it operates at peak performance. This includes cleaning the lenses and mirrors to prevent distortion of the laser beam, checking the alignment of the laser for consistent engraving across the material, and replacing parts that show signs of wear.

Lastly, continuous learning and experimentation play a significant role in improving engraving quality. The world of laser engraving is constantly evolving, with new techniques, materials, and technologies emerging. Staying informed through online forums, tutorials, and community workshops can provide valuable insights and inspiration.

By paying attention to these advanced tips and continually refining your approach, you can enhance the quality of your laser engravings, turning simple projects into works of art. Remember, every engraver has unique qualities, and mastering your machine's specific characteristics is key to unlocking its full potential.

Maintenance and Care of Your Laser Engraver

Daily and Weekly Maintenance Routines

Maintaining a laser engraver is crucial for ensuring its longevity, efficiency, and the quality of the engravings it produces. For beginners, establishing daily and weekly maintenance routines can seem daunting, but these practices become second nature with time and significantly contribute to the seamless operation of the equipment. Proper maintenance routines not only prevent downtime and costly repairs but also ensure the safety of the operator.

Daily maintenance routines are the cornerstone of laser engraver care. Each day before starting the machine, it's essential to check the laser engraving area for any debris or remnants from previous projects. Removing these ensures a clean workspace and prevents any interference with the laser's path, which can affect the quality of the engraving or even damage the machine. Inspecting and cleaning the focusing lens is another critical daily task. Since the lens focuses the laser beam, any residue or dust can diffuse the laser's focus, leading to uneven or poor-quality engravings. Using a soft, lint-free cloth and lens cleaner designed for optical surfaces can prevent scratches and remove any buildup effectively.

The condition of the laser's mirrors also demands daily attention. These mirrors direct the laser beam to the material being engraved. If they are misaligned or dirty, the laser's path can be altered, affecting the engraving precision. Gently cleaning the mirrors with a proper cleaning solution and a microfiber cloth can prevent these issues. It's also beneficial to check the air assist compressor daily if your machine is equipped with one. Ensuring that the air assist is clean and functioning correctly helps remove debris from the cutting area, maintains a clear path for the laser, and reduces the risk of fire.

Weekly maintenance routines dive deeper into the care of the laser engraver. This includes a thorough check of the engraver's ventilation system. The extraction system or fume extractor plays a pivotal role in removing harmful fumes and debris generated during the engraving process. Cleaning or replacing the filters as needed ensures that the machine operates in a safe environment and prevents buildup that could restrict airflow or reduce the effectiveness of fume extraction.

Another weekly task is to inspect the laser bed or cutting table. Over time, the table can accumulate residue or become damaged from the heat and pressure of the laser. Cleaning the table and checking for any signs of wear or damage can prevent defects in the materials being engraved and extend the life of the bed. For machines with a honeycomb cutting bed, removing any trapped debris from the crevices is also necessary to maintain optimal airflow and engraving quality.

Lubricating the moving parts of the laser engraver, such as the rails and bearings, is a weekly routine that shouldn't be overlooked. Applying the correct type of lubricant according to the manufacturer's recommendations ensures smooth operation and prevents wear and tear on these crucial components.

Regularly updating the laser engraver's software forms part of a comprehensive maintenance routine. Software updates can enhance the machine's performance, introduce new features, and fix any known bugs. Checking for and installing software updates weekly ensures that the engraver operates with the latest improvements and security patches.

Cleaning and Replacing the Laser Lens

Maintaining the laser lens is critical for ensuring the longevity and efficiency of a laser engraver. A clean lens ensures optimal focus, precision, and quality of the engraved product, while a damaged or worn lens can lead to poor engraving results and potential harm to the machine. For beginners, understanding the process of cleaning and replacing the laser lens is essential to keep the laser engraver in top condition.

The lens of a laser engraver focuses the laser beam onto the material's surface. Over time, debris such as dust, resin, and other contaminants from the engraving process can accumulate on the lens. This accumulation can distort the laser beam, resulting in uneven engraving or, in worse cases, preventing the laser from cutting or engraving altogether. Regular cleaning of the lens is therefore necessary to maintain the quality of work and prevent damage to the machine.

To clean the laser lens, first, ensure that the laser engraver is turned off and completely cool. Safety should always be the priority, so wearing protective gloves and eyewear is recommended to protect against accidental injury. Begin by accessing the lens following the manufacturer's instructions. This usually involves opening the laser engraver's casing and carefully removing the lens holder.

Once the lens is accessible, use a lens cleaning solution specifically designed for laser engravers. Apply a few drops of the solution onto a lens cleaning tissue or a lint-free cloth. Gently wipe the lens in a circular motion, starting from the center and moving outward. This method helps to avoid scratching the lens and ensures that any debris is not dragged across the surface of the lens. It is crucial to avoid using rough materials or excessive force, as the lens is delicate and can be easily damaged.

After cleaning, inspect the lens for any signs of damage such as scratches, chips, or cloudiness. If the lens is damaged, it will need to be replaced to ensure the laser engraver functions correctly. Continuing to use a damaged lens can result in poor engraving quality and may also cause further damage to the machine.

Replacing the laser lens involves selecting the appropriate lens for your laser engraver. Lenses come in different focal lengths, which are suited for various engraving tasks. Consult the manufacturer's recommendations to choose the correct lens for your specific engraving needs. To replace the lens, carefully remove the old lens from the holder, avoiding touching the new lens's surface with your fingers, as oils and dirt can affect its performance. Place the new lens in the holder and secure it according to the manufacturer's instructions.

After replacing the lens, it's a good practice to perform a test engraving on a scrap piece of material. This allows you to check the quality of the engraving and make any necessary adjustments to the machine settings.

Regular maintenance of the laser lens is a crucial aspect of laser engraver care. Beginners should familiarize themselves with the cleaning and replacement process to ensure their machine remains in optimal working condition. Scheduling regular cleaning sessions, depending on the frequency of use and the types of materials engraved, will help maintain the quality of engravings and extend the life of the laser engraver. Proper care and maintenance not only protect your investment but also ensure that your creative projects are always of the highest quality.

Maintaining the Laser Tube

Maintaining the laser tube is crucial for ensuring the longevity and efficiency of a laser engraver. This component is at the heart of the machine, generating the laser beam that etches designs into various materials. For beginners, understanding how to care for the laser tube can seem daunting, but with the right knowledge and practices, it becomes a manageable and essential part of routine maintenance.

The first step in maintaining the laser tube is to keep it clean. Dust, debris, and residue can accumulate on the tube, potentially obstructing the laser beam's path and diminishing the engraver's performance. Cleaning the tube regularly with a soft, lint-free cloth and isopropyl alcohol can prevent buildup. It's important to handle the tube gently to avoid damage, ensuring that any cleaning agents used do not degrade the tube's material.

Water cooling systems are often used in conjunction with laser tubes to regulate their temperature during operation. Ensuring that this cooling system functions correctly is vital for preventing the laser tube from overheating, which can cause permanent damage and reduce its lifespan. Regularly check the water level, quality, and flow rate. Using distilled water is recommended to prevent mineral buildup inside the cooling system. If a water chiller is used, keeping it clean and free from obstructions ensures efficient cooling.

Monitoring the laser tube's temperature is also crucial. Operating the laser engraver in an environment with stable, moderate temperatures helps prevent thermal stress on the tube. Extreme temperature fluctuations can cause the materials in the tube to expand and contract, leading to cracks or other damages. Implementing a consistent temperature control in the workspace can significantly extend the tube's operational life.

Another aspect of maintaining the laser tube is checking for signs of wear or damage, such as cracks, discoloration, or a noticeable decrease in performance. These signs could indicate that the tube is nearing the end of its life or requires professional inspection. Recognizing these symptoms early can prevent more significant issues down the line, ensuring that replacements or repairs are carried out before the machine's functionality is compromised.

Calibration plays a significant role in maintaining the laser tube's efficiency. Ensuring that the laser beam is correctly aligned within the engraver's optical path maximizes the tube's output and prevents uneven wear. Periodic checks and adjustments, according to the manufacturer's guidelines, help maintain optimal performance. This might include cleaning and aligning mirrors and lenses that focus and direct the laser beam, as improperly aligned optics can strain the tube and degrade the quality of engravings.

Finally, maintaining a usage log for the laser tube can help track its performance and anticipate maintenance needs. Logging hours of operation, cleaning schedules, temperature conditions, and any adjustments or repairs provides valuable data that can inform maintenance practices. This proactive approach allows users to anticipate when the tube might require attention, based on its usage patterns and historical performance.

For beginners, maintaining the laser tube may initially appear as an intricate part of laser engraver upkeep. However, by incorporating these practices into regular maintenance routines, users can significantly enhance their engraver's performance and lifespan. Proper care of the laser tube not only ensures the machine operates at its best but also safeguards the user's investment, enabling the creation of high-quality engravings for years to come.

Troubleshooting Mechanical Issues

Troubleshooting mechanical issues in a laser engraver requires a systematic approach, especially for beginners. When your machine starts acting up, it might feel overwhelming, but understanding common problems and their solutions can help keep your laser engraver running smoothly.

One of the first issues many new users encounter is a decrease in the quality of the engraving. This can often be traced back to a dirty or damaged lens. The lens focuses the laser beam onto the material, and even a small amount of debris can distort the beam's path, leading to unclear engravings. Cleaning the lens with a recommended cleaning solution and a lint-free cloth can resolve this issue. If the lens is scratched or damaged, it will need to be replaced.

Another common problem is misalignment of the laser beam, which can result in uneven engraving depth or the laser not hitting the intended target area at all. This usually happens after prolonged use or if the machine has been moved or bumped. Most laser engravers have built-in alignment procedures detailed in the user manual. Following these steps carefully can realign the laser beam. For some models, this might involve adjusting mirrors that reflect the laser beam to the lens. It's crucial to handle these components gently to avoid damage.

Belts and gears drive the movement of the laser head. Over time, these can become loose or wear out, leading to inaccuracies in engraving. Checking for any slackness in the belts and tightening them according to the manufacturer's specifications can improve performance. Gears should be checked for any debris that might be causing blockages and cleaned accordingly. If wear and tear are evident, replacing these parts is necessary to maintain the machine's accuracy.

The quality of engravings can also be affected by an uncalibrated or dirty z-axis, which controls the up-and-down movement of the laser head or the material bed. This is particularly true for laser engravers that require manual focus adjustments. Regularly calibrating the z-axis and ensuring it moves smoothly without obstruction can prevent issues related to focus and depth of the engraving.

Temperature fluctuations within the laser engraver can lead to mechanical issues as well. Laser engravers generate a significant amount of heat during operation, and if the cooling system is not working efficiently, it can lead to overheating. This can cause the machine to shut down mid-operation or, worse, damage sensitive components. Ensuring that the cooling system, whether air or water-based, is functioning correctly is essential. This includes checking for any blockages in air vents, replacing coolant fluid regularly, and ensuring water pumps are operational for water-cooled systems.

For beginners experiencing issues with their laser engraver, it's also worthwhile to check the power supply and control board. Fluctuations in power can cause erratic behavior or even prevent the machine from turning on. Ensuring your setup is connected to a stable power source and checking for any loose connections can solve these issues. If the machine experiences frequent power interruptions, using a surge protector or uninterruptible power supply (UPS) can provide stability.

Software plays a significant role in the operation of a laser engraver, and while not a mechanical issue per se, problems with software can manifest in the physical performance of the machine. Ensuring that the software is up to date, properly configured for the machine, and free from bugs can help prevent issues that appear to be mechanical but are actually software-related.

Lastly, regular maintenance is key to preventing mechanical issues. This includes cleaning all components of the laser engraver, lubricating moving parts, and checking for wear and tear on a regular basis. Keeping a log of maintenance activities can help track when parts were last cleaned, adjusted, or replaced, making it easier to diagnose issues when they arise.

For beginners, understanding and troubleshooting mechanical issues with a laser engraver might seem daunting at first. However, with patience, a methodical approach, and a willingness to learn from each problem, maintaining a laser engraver can become a manageable part of the creative process.

Creative Projects to Get You Started

Simple Projects for Beginners

Embarking on the journey of laser engraving opens up a world of creative possibilities, offering beginners an exciting way to explore their artistic abilities and technical skills. Starting with simple projects allows newcomers to become familiar with their laser engraver's capabilities while producing rewarding and tangible results. These projects serve as the building blocks for more complex endeavors and can be tailored to fit personal interests or gift-giving occasions.

One of the first projects often recommended is custom keychains. Keychains are small, easy to design, and require minimal material, making them perfect for beginners. By engraving names, initials, or simple icons onto wood, acrylic, or leather, beginners can practice adjusting the laser's power settings and speed. This project offers instant gratification and a useful introduction to working with different materials.

Another great starting point is creating personalized coasters. Coasters are practical items for everyday use and can be made from wood, acrylic, or slate. Beginners can experiment with geometric patterns, family initials, or small quotes. This project helps in understanding how to control the laser for deeper cuts or more superficial etches, depending on the desired visual effect and the material's properties.

For those interested in home decor, engraved wooden signs offer a fantastic canvas to work on. Starting with simple designs such as welcome signs, quotes, or family names, beginners can learn how to manage larger pieces of material and how to evenly distribute the laser's focus across a broader surface. Wooden signs also allow for experimentation with different fonts and detailed designs, enhancing a beginner's confidence in design preparation and execution.

Book lovers might enjoy personalizing bookmarks. Using thin wood or leather, beginners can engrave intricate designs, literary quotes, or even images using raster engraving techniques. This project introduces the concept of layering designs and adjusting the laser for fine detail work, skills that are essential for more advanced projects.

Custom engraved glasses or mugs can be an exciting challenge for beginners ready to explore etching on glass or ceramic surfaces. Starting with simple patterns or text, users can practice creating stencils and adjusting the laser for etching on curved surfaces. This project not only expands the range of materials one is comfortable working with but also introduces the importance of proper material preparation and post-processing for clean, crisp designs.

For a more personal touch, creating photo frames with custom messages or designs offers a blend of technical and artistic skills. Beginners can learn how to integrate text with decorative elements, balance a design aesthetically, and work with larger pieces of material. This project enhances understanding of layout considerations and material properties, providing a solid foundation for more complex designs.

Lastly, making personalized business cards out of wood or acrylic is an innovative way to test one's skills. This project requires precision and attention to detail, as the text must be legible and the overall design aesthetically pleasing. It's an excellent way to get accustomed to working with very thin fonts and intricate logos, as well as understanding how different speeds and power settings affect the material.

These simple projects for beginners not only offer the satisfaction of creating something beautiful and functional but also equip novice users with the knowledge and skills needed to tackle more complex laser engraving projects. Through trial, error, and experimentation, beginners can gradually build their confidence, understanding the nuances of laser engraving, and eventually, transform their creative ideas into reality.

Intermediate Projects to Explore

- Delving into intermediate projects with a laser engraver opens up a new realm of creativity and technical prowess, allowing beginners to stretch their skills and explore the extensive capabilities of their machines. After mastering the basics of laser engraving, such as simple cuts and etchings on materials like wood and acrylic, enthusiasts are often eager to tackle more challenging projects. These endeavors not only enhance one's engraving skills but also result in captivating pieces that stand out for their complexity and craftsmanship.

One exciting intermediate project is the creation of layered 3D models. This process involves engraving and cutting several layers of material, usually wood or acrylic, and then stacking them to form a three-dimensional model. The intricacy of these projects lies in the precision required to ensure that all layers align perfectly. Engravers can create topographical maps, architectural models, or any scene that benefits from depth and dimension. The key is to gradually increase layer complexity, starting with simpler designs and advancing to more detailed landscapes or intricate patterns.

Custom puzzles offer another avenue for intermediate laser engravers to showcase their skills. By using the laser to cut unique puzzle shapes out of wood or acrylic, creators can fashion bespoke puzzles featuring personalized images or patterns. The challenge here is in designing the puzzle pieces themselves—a task that demands both creativity and an understanding of spatial relationships. Advanced software can assist in generating the puzzle cut lines from a chosen image, providing a seamless transition from digital design to tangible product.

Engraving detailed artwork onto mixed materials is a project that tests both the artist's and the machine's finesse. By combining materials with different properties, such as wood with metal or glass with leather, engravers can produce works that are not only visually striking but also textured. The difficulty in this project lies in adjusting the laser's settings to suit each material's engraving requirements, ensuring that the final piece showcases the intended detail and depth without damaging the materials.

Personalized jewelry and accessories take the personalization capability of laser engravers to a new level. Intermediate users can engrave intricate designs or text onto metal pendants, leather bracelets, or wooden earrings. The precision required for these smaller items demands a steady hand in design preparation and an acute understanding of how different materials react to the laser's heat. These projects not only refine the user's ability to work with small, delicate items but also open up possibilities for custom fashion lines or personalized gifts.

Incorporating electronics into laser-cut projects is a venture into the merging worlds of technology and art. Enthusiasts can create wooden boxes with engraved details that house electronic components, such as LED lights, to add functionality to their aesthetic appeal. This requires a basic understanding of electronics alongside engraving skills, presenting a multidisciplinary challenge that rewards with uniquely interactive creations.

Functional home decor, such as engraved lampshades or intricate clock faces, pushes the envelope of what's possible with a laser engraver. These projects not only serve a practical purpose but also act as a canvas for showcasing the beauty of laser-cut designs. The challenge lies in integrating artistic elements with functional design, ensuring that the final product is both beautiful and useful.

Venturing into these intermediate projects with a laser engraver encourages users to explore the limits of their creativity and technical skills. Each project builds on the fundamentals learned from simpler tasks, gradually introducing more complex techniques and materials. As engravers navigate through these challenges, they not only enhance their capabilities but also uncover the vast potential for innovation that laser engraving technology offers.

Advanced Project Ideas

When you've mastered the basics of laser engraving, the door to more complex and innovative projects swings wide open. Advancing beyond simple designs and materials, these projects challenge your creativity and technical skills, pushing the boundaries of what's possible with a laser engraver. Here, we explore a selection of advanced project ideas that not only inspire but also refine your engraving capabilities.

Creating layered 3D models is an ambitious start. By engraving and cutting multiple layers of material, such as wood or acrylic, and then stacking them, you can create intricate 3D models. These models can range from detailed cityscapes to complex anatomical figures, offering a stunning visual impact. This technique requires precise design planning and alignment during the assembly process, making it a perfect challenge for those looking to level up their skills.

Personalized puzzles offer a unique twist on a classic pastime. With a laser engraver, you can transform photographs or intricate artwork into wooden or acrylic puzzles. The complexity of these puzzles can be adjusted by varying the size and shape of the puzzle pieces, and the personal touch makes them exceptional gifts or keepsakes. This project tests your ability to manage both the aesthetic aspects of the design and the functional fit of the puzzle pieces.

Custom inlay work is another area where laser engraving shines. By precisely engraving the recesses on one piece of material and cutting complementary inlays from another, you can create stunning patterns or images with depth and contrast. This technique can be applied to furniture, musical instruments, or decorative panels, demanding a high degree of accuracy and attention to detail in both design and execution.

Illuminated signs and artworks open up a realm of possibilities by combining laser-engraved designs with lighting. By engraving on translucent materials like acrylic and backing them with LED lights, you can create eye-catching signs, nightlights, or art pieces that glow with a soft, ambient light. This project not only tests your engraving skills but also your ability to work with lighting and electronics, offering a multidisciplinary challenge.

Wearable art, such as engraved jewelry or accessory pieces, allows you to bring your laser engraving skills into the fashion world. Using metals, leather, or wood, you can create intricate designs that can be worn. This application requires a delicate touch, as the materials are often more challenging to work with, and the scale of the designs is smaller. However, the end result is a wearable piece of art that showcases the versatility of laser engraving.

Interactive art installations invite audience participation and engagement, taking laser engraving into the public sphere. By incorporating engraved elements into larger installations, you can create pieces that respond to or change with viewer interaction. This might include engraved panels that cast intricate shadows, components that move or change appearance, or interactive puzzles that visitors can solve. These projects not only showcase your technical skills but also your ability to think creatively about the viewer's experience.

In crafting these advanced projects, patience, precision, and a willingness to experiment are key. Each project not only challenges your understanding of the laser engraving process but also encourages you to think creatively about design, materials, and the possibilities of the medium. As you tackle these complex projects, you'll find that the laser engraver is not just a tool, but a partner in your creative journey, opening up a world of possibilities for what you can create and imagine.

Conclusion

Embarking on the journey of mastering a laser engraver as a beginner might seem daunting at first. Yet, through this exploration, what emerges is not just an understanding of a complex tool but a gateway to unleashing creative potential in ways one might never have imagined. The process of learning to use a laser engraver, from the initial steps of understanding its mechanics and safety procedures to executing complex projects, is both enriching and empowering.

At the heart of this journey is the realization that laser engraving is much more than a technical skill. It is an art form that blends technology with creativity, offering endless possibilities for personalization, artistic expression, and functional creation. The ability to transform a simple piece of material into something beautiful, meaningful, or practical is a powerful experience, one that enriches not only the maker but also those who come into contact with their work.

As beginners progress from simple projects to more advanced creations, they develop not just technical proficiency but also a deeper understanding of the materials they work with and the ways in which their unique properties can be harnessed and highlighted. This journey encourages a mindset of experimentation and learning, where each mistake becomes a lesson and every success paves the way for new challenges.

Moreover, the skills acquired through mastering laser engraving have implications far beyond personal satisfaction and artistic fulfillment. They open doors to entrepreneurial opportunities, educational applications, and community engagement, allowing individuals to share their skills, collaborate with others, and contribute to a growing community of makers and creators.

In conclusion, the journey of learning how to use a laser engraver is about much more than mastering a piece of equipment. It is about discovering a new medium for expression, innovation, and connection. It invites individuals to see the world around them through a lens of potential - where every surface becomes a canvas and every idea has the possibility of being brought to life. For those willing to embark on this journey, the rewards are as boundless as their creativity, offering not just a new set of skills but a new way of engaging with the world.

www.ingramcontent.com/pod-product-compliance
Lightning Source LLC
Chambersburg PA
CBHW070155230526
45471CB00002B/671